TRANSPORT PICTURES

SHAMBHALA AGILE RABBIT EDITIONS

BOSTON

1999

TRANSPORT PICTURES

Shambhala Publications, Inc.
Horticultural Hall
300 Massachusetts Avenue
Bostzon, Massachusetts 02115
http://www.shambhala.com

987654321
Printed in Singapore
∞ This edition is printed on acid-free paper that meets the American National Standards
Institute z39.48 Standard.
Distributed in the United States by Random House, Inc., and in Canada by Random House
of Canada Ltd

See page 8 for Cataloging-in-Publication data

Other books with CD-ROM by Shambhala Agile Rabbit Editions:

ISBN 1-57062-477-1	Batik Patterns
ISBN 1-57062-480-1	Chinese Patterns
ISBN 1-57062-483-6	Decorated Initials
ISBN 1-57062-478-x	Floral Patterns
ISBN 1-57062-484-4	Graphic Frames
ISBN 1-57062-479-8	Images of The Human Body
ISBN 1-57062-482-8	Sports Pictures

Library of Congress Cataloging-in-Publication Data

Transport Pictures / [compiled by Pepin van Roojen].
        p.   cm.
    ISBN 1-57062-481-x (alk. paper)
    1. Transportation in art.   2. Decoration and ornament.   3. Clip
art.   I. Roojen, Pepin van.
NK1590.T73T74 1999
704.9'49388–dc21   99-19170
                                                    CIP

This book contains high-quality images for use as a graphic resource or inspiration. All the images are stored on the accompanying CD-ROM in professional quality, high-resolution format and can be used on either Windows or Mac platforms. The images can be used free of charge.

The documents can be imported directly from the CD-ROM into a wide range of layout, image-manipulation, illustration, and word-processing programs; no installation is required. Many programs allow you to manipulate the images. Please consult your software manual for further instructions.

The names of the files on the CD-ROM correspond with the page numbers in this book. Where applicable, the position on the pages is indicated: T = top, B = bottom, C = center, L = left, and R = right.

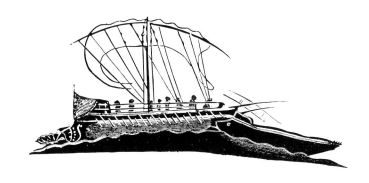

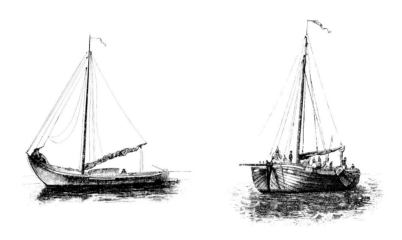

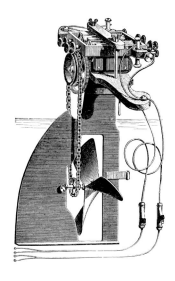

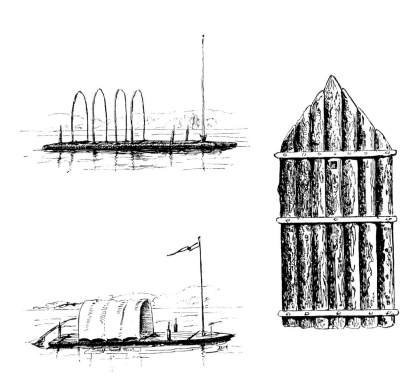

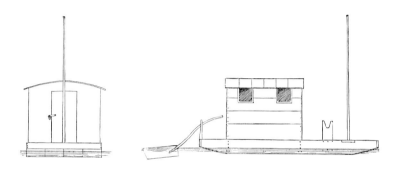

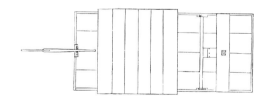

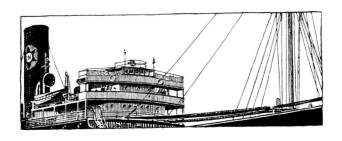

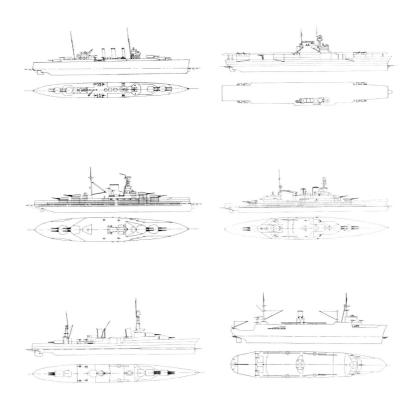

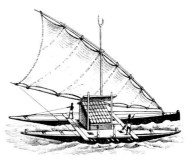

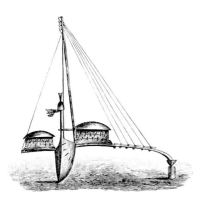

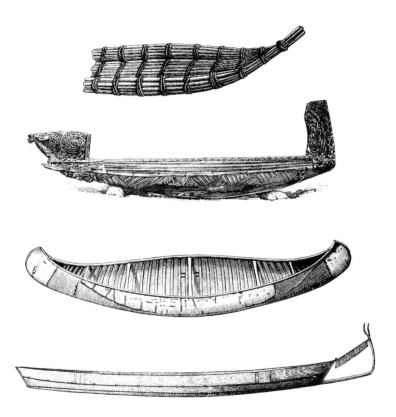

43

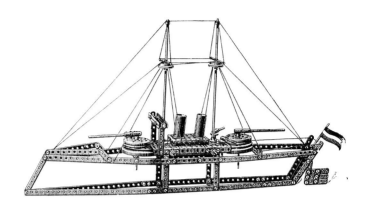

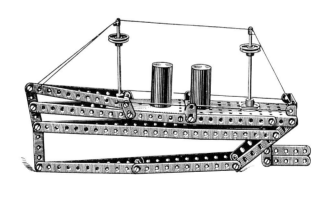

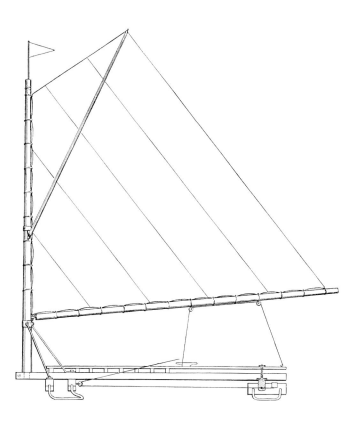

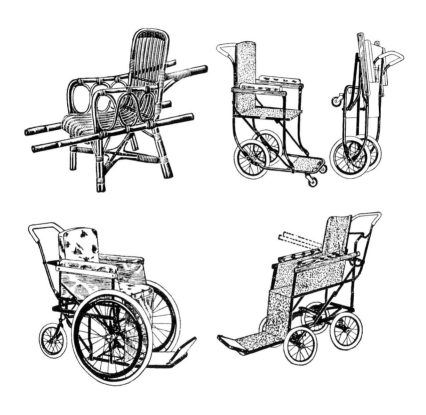

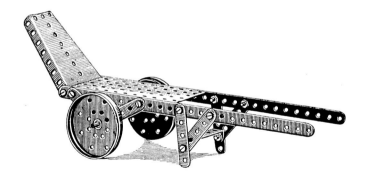

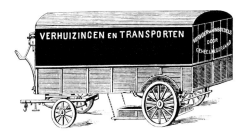

VERHUIZINGEN EN TRANSPORTEN

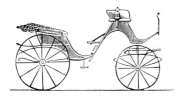

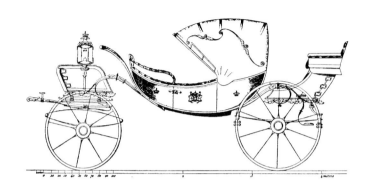

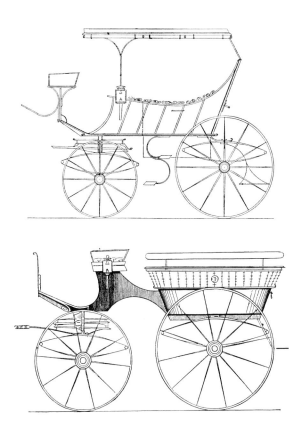

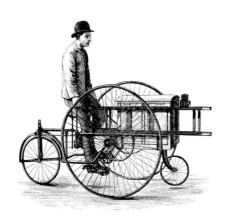

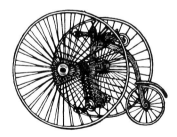

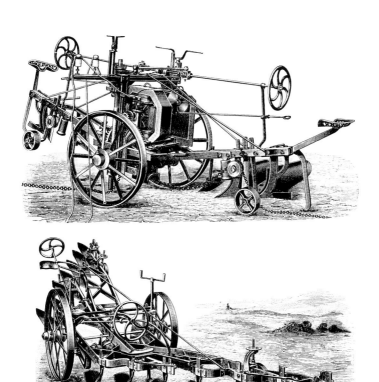

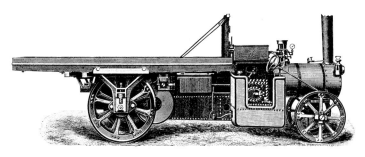

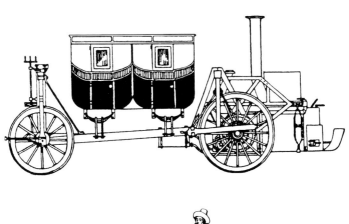

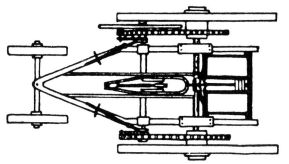

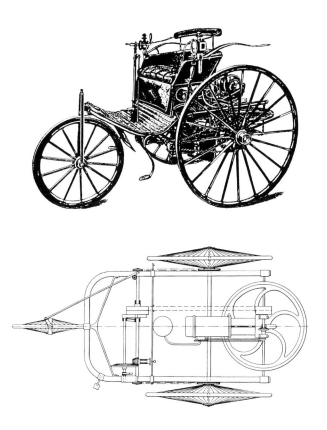

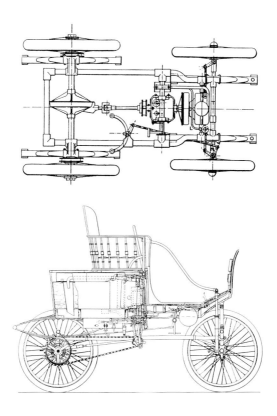

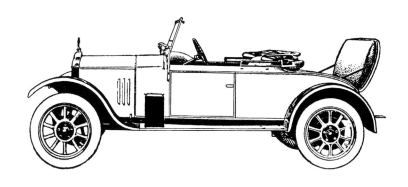

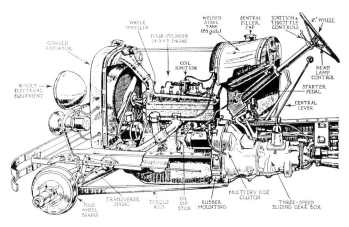

WATER IMPELLER
WELDED STEEL TANK (8½ galls)
CENTRAL FILLER CAP
IGNITION & THROTTLE CONTROLS
18" WHEEL
FOUR-CYLINDER 14·9 H.P. ENGINE
COWLED RADIATOR
COIL IGNITION
HEAD LAMP CONTROL
6-VOLT ELECTRICAL EQUIPMENT
STARTER PEDAL
CENTRAL LEVER
FOUR WHEEL BRAKES
TRANSVERSE SPRING
TORQUE ROD
OIL DIP STICK
RUBBER MOUNTING
MULTI DRY DISC CLUTCH
THREE-SPEED SLIDING GEAR BOX

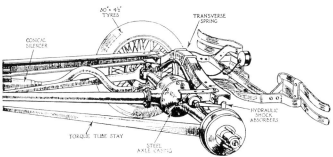

30" × 4½" TYRES
TRANSVERSE SPRING
CONICAL SILENCER
HYDRAULIC SHOCK ABSORBERS
TORQUE TUBE STAY
STEEL AXLE CASING

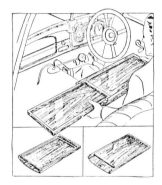

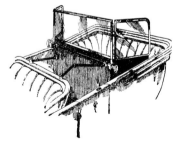

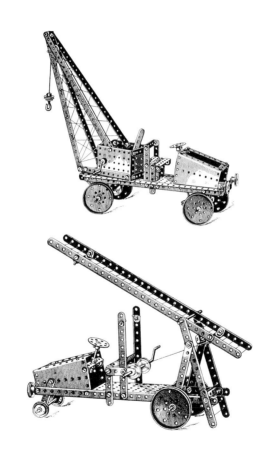

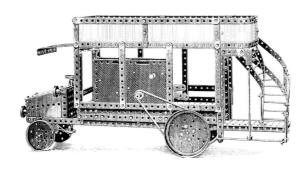

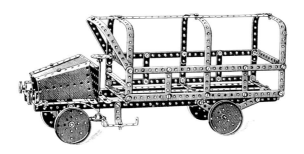

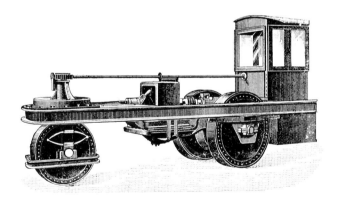

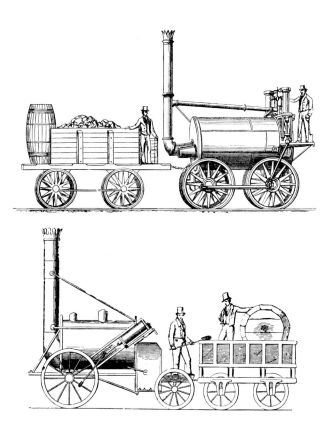

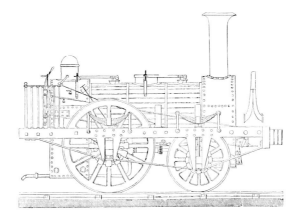

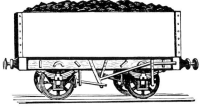

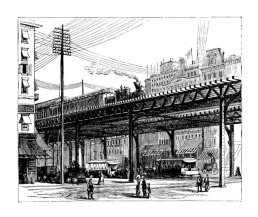

179

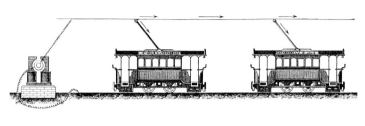

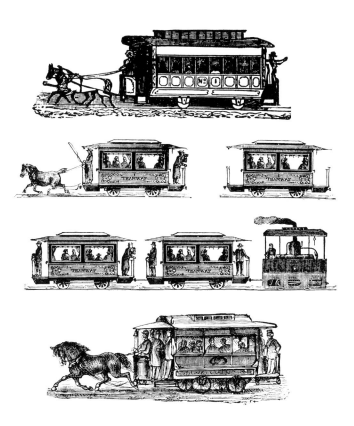

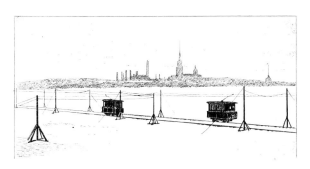

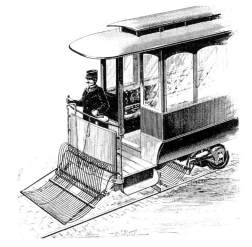

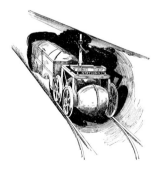

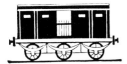

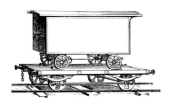
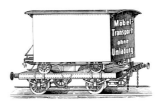

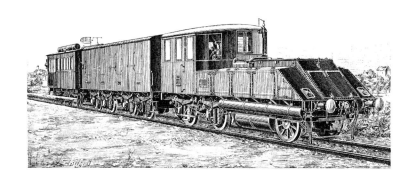

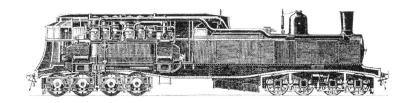

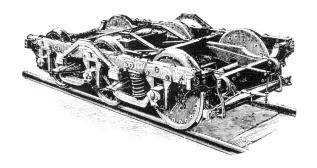

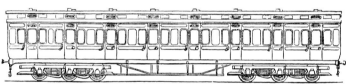

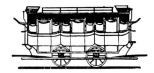

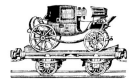

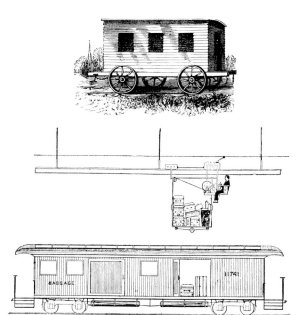

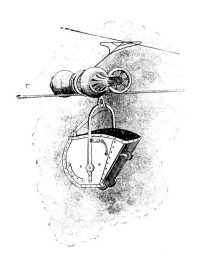

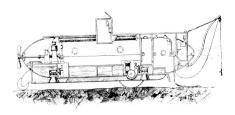

199

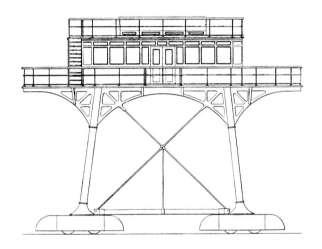

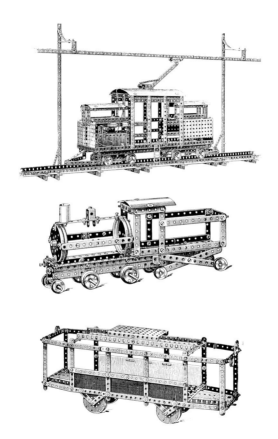

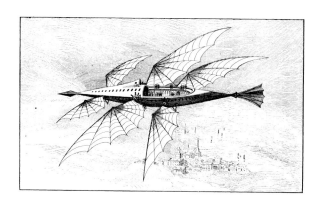

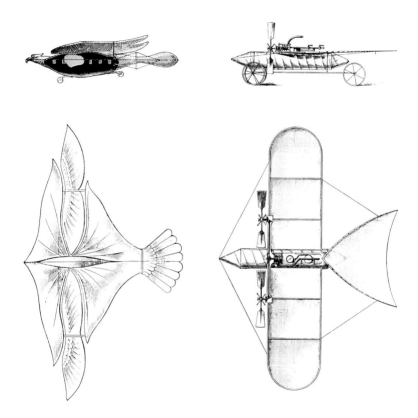

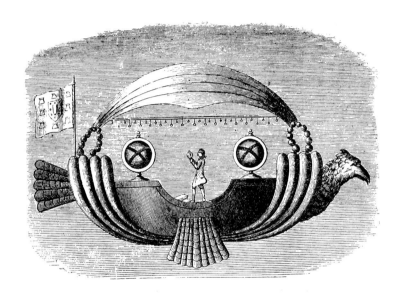

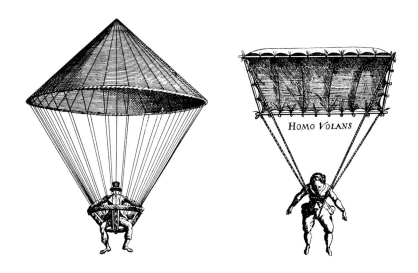

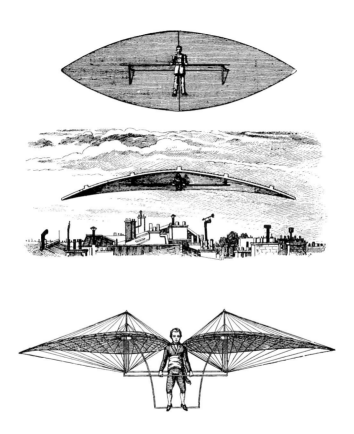

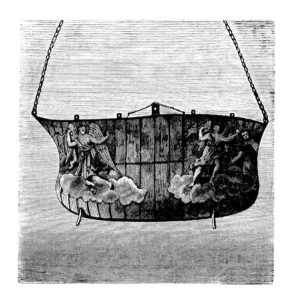

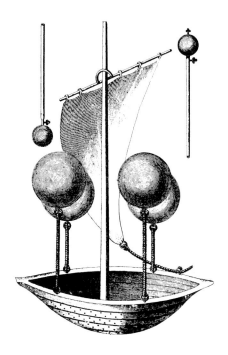

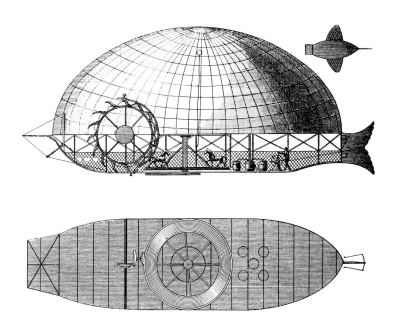

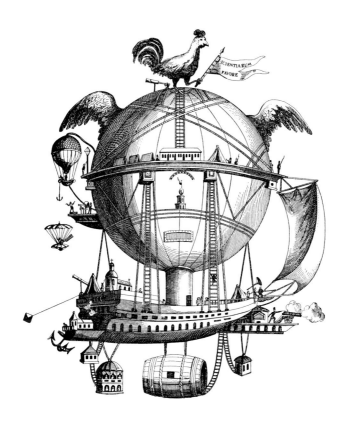

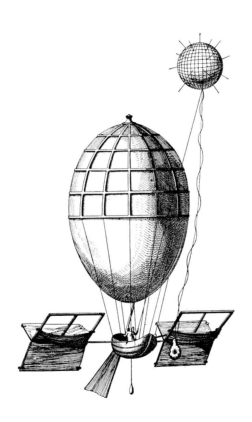

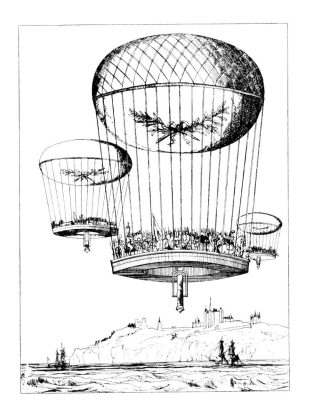

219

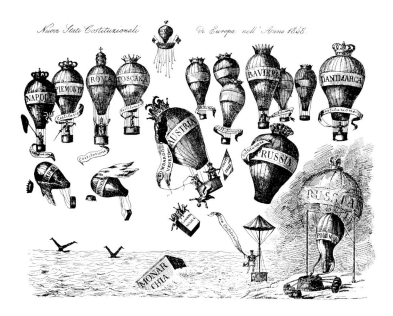

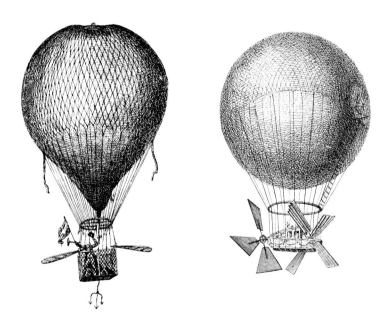

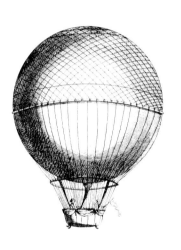

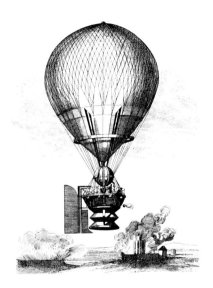

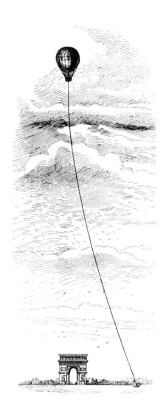

232

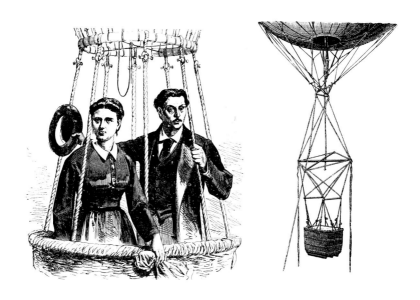

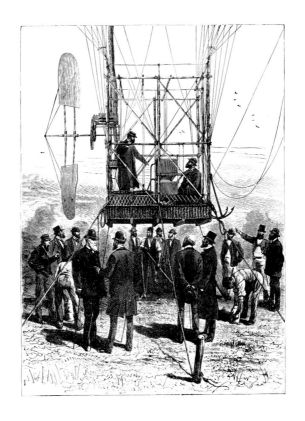

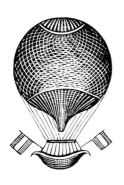

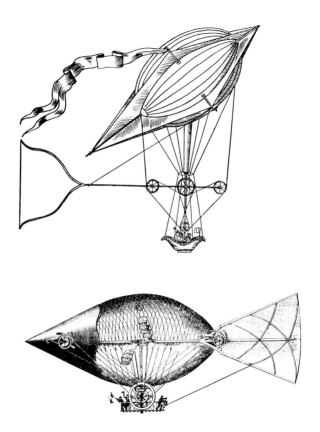

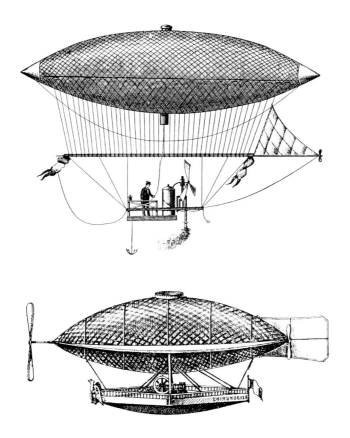

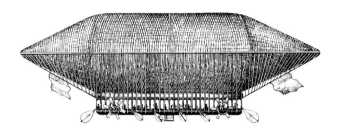

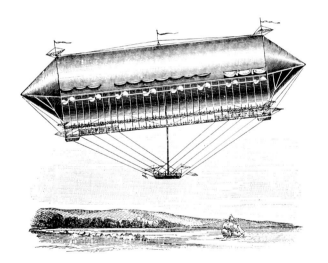

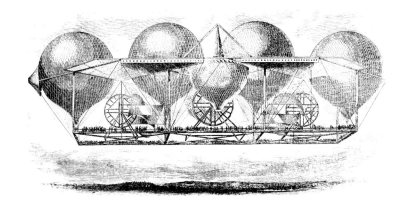

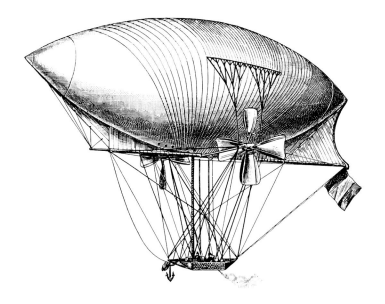

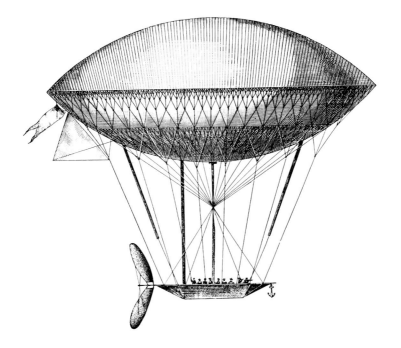

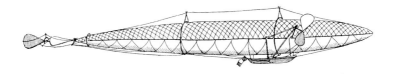

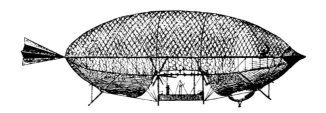

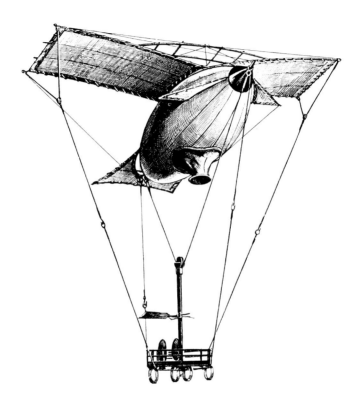

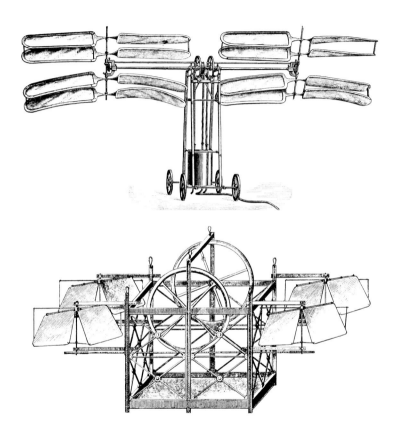

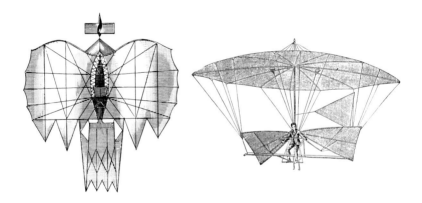

254

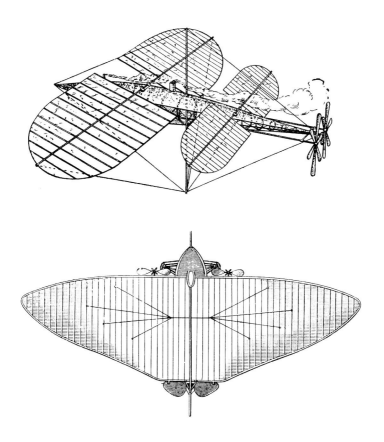

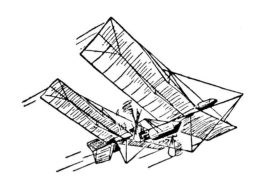

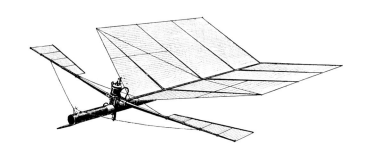

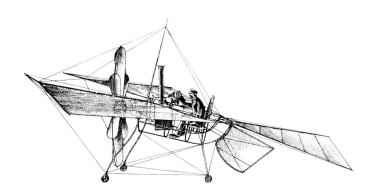

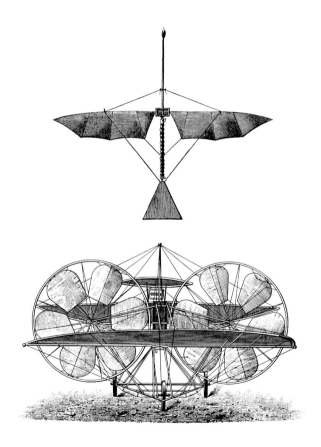

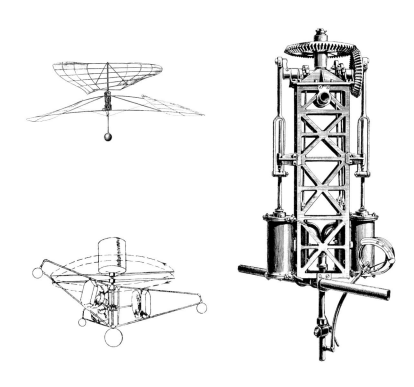

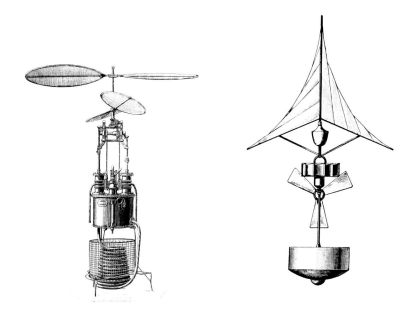

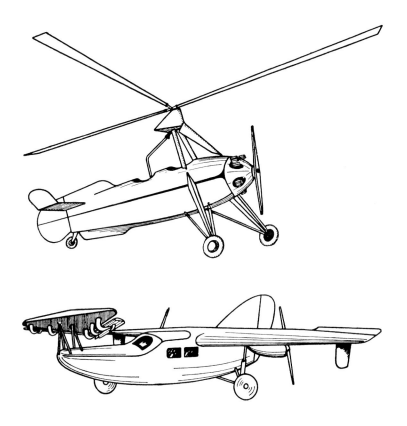

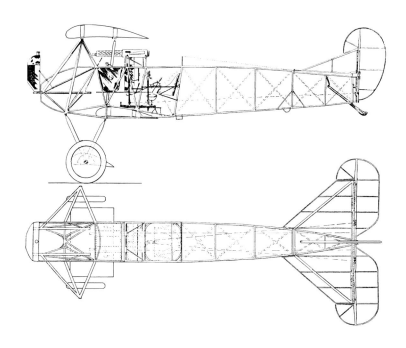

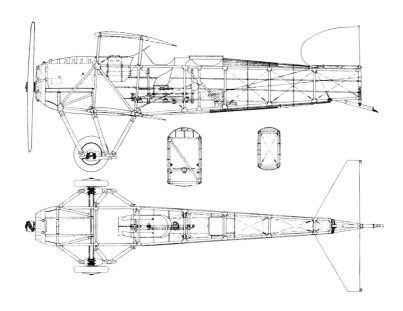

265

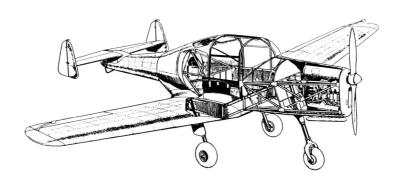

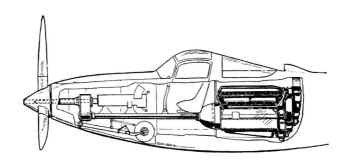

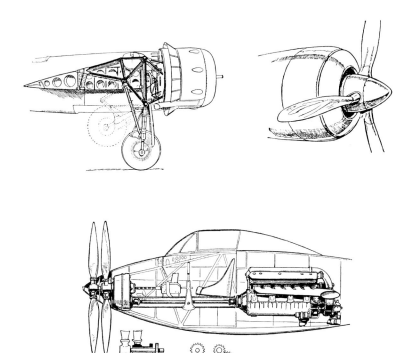

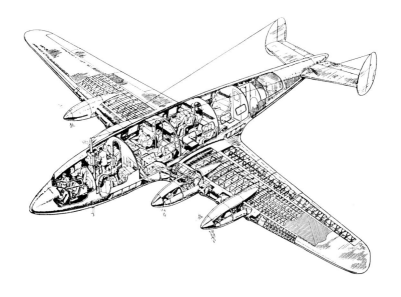

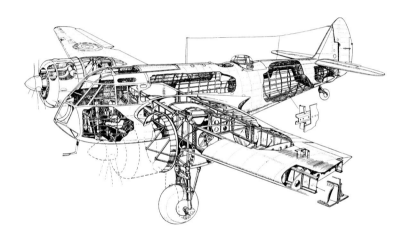

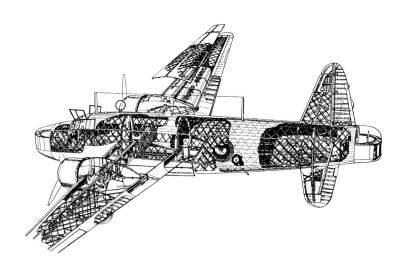

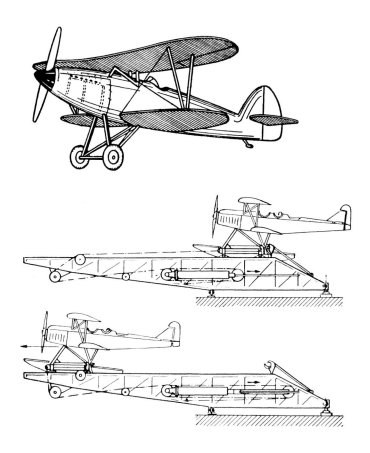

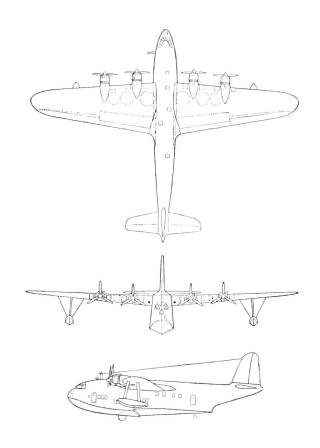

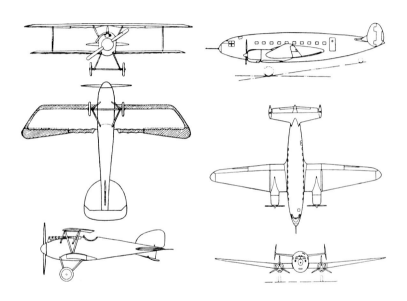

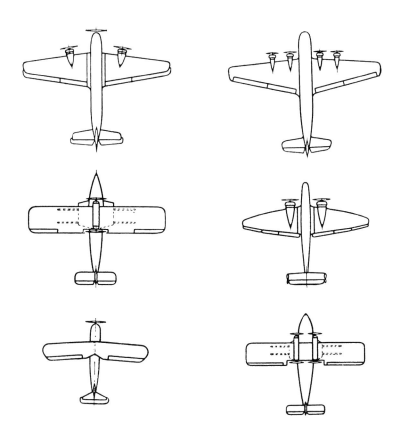

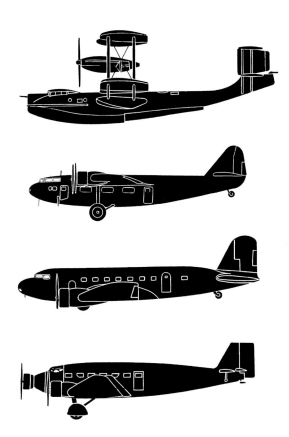

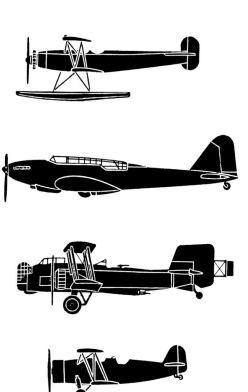

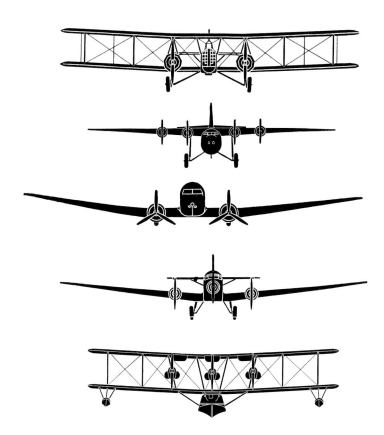

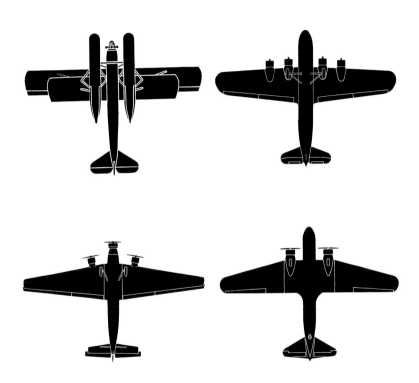

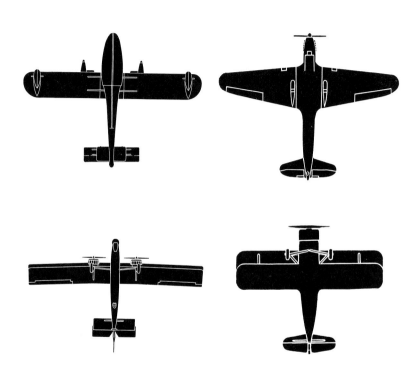

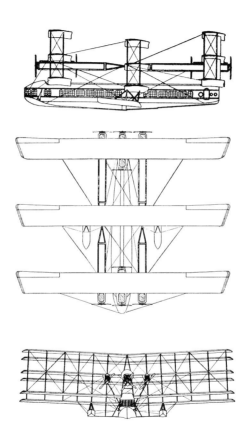

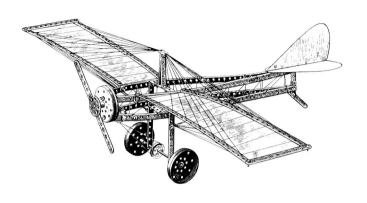

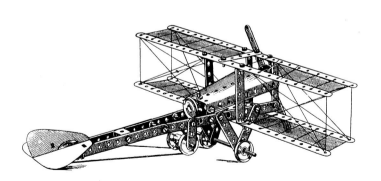

NEW SAREPTA HIGH SCHOOL

Other books with free CD-ROM by Shambhala Agile Rabbit Editions:

ISBN 1-57062-477-1   Batik Patterns
ISBN 1-57062-480-1   Chinese Patterns
ISBN 1-57062-483-6   Decorated Initials
ISBN 1-57062-478-x   Floral Patterns
ISBN 1-57062-484-4   Graphic Frames
ISBN 1-57062-479-8   Images of The Human Body
ISBN 1-57062-482-8   Sports Pictures

Shambhala Publications, Inc.
Horticultural Hall
300 Massachusetts Avenue
Boston, Massachusetts 02115
http://www.shambhala.com

987654321
Printed in Singapore
∞ This edition is printed on acid-free paper that meets the American National Standards Institute z39.48 Standard.
Distributed in the United States by Random House, Inc., and in Canada by Random House of Canada Ltd

Library of Congress Cataloging-in-Publication Data

Transport Pictures / [compiled by Pepin van Roojen].
       p.   cm.
    ISBN 1-57062-481-x (alk. paper)
    1. Transportation in art.   2. Decoration and ornament.   3. Clip
art.   I. Roojen, Pepin van.
NK1590.T73T74 1999
704.9'49388–dc21   99-19170
                                                                     CIP